HOW-TO
LIBRARY

LEARNING TO CROCHET

By Dana Meachen Rau • Illustrated by Kathleen Petelinsek

CHERRY LAKE PUB   ARBOR, MICHIGAN

Published in the United States of America by Cherry Lake Publishing
Ann Arbor, Michigan
www.cherrylakepublishing.com

Photo Credits: Page 4, ©Es75/Shutterstock; page 5, ©lcrms/Shutterstock; page 6, ©Andreea Dragomir/Shutterstock; page 7, ©blue caterpillar/Shutterstock; page 8, ©okanakdeniz/Shutterstock; page 9, ©Melica/Shutterstock; page 29, ©Ekaterina Kamenetsky/Shutterstock; page 32, ©Charlie Rau.

Library of Congress Cataloging-in-Publication Data
Names: Rau, Dana Meachen, 1971- author.
Title: Learning to crochet / by Dana Meachen Rau.
Description: Ann Arbor, Michigan : Cherry Lake Publishing, [2016] |
    Series: How-to library. Crafts | Audience: Grades 4 to 6. |
    Includes bibliographical references and index.
Identifiers: LCCN 2015048728 | ISBN 9781634714181 (lib. bdg.) |
ISBN 9781634714341 (pbk.) | ISBN 9781634714266 (pdf) |
ISBN 9781634714426 (ebook)
Subjects: LCSH: Crocheting—Juvenile literature.
Classification: LCC TT820 .R374 2016 | DDC 746.43/4—dc23
LC record available at http://lccn.loc.gov/2015048728

Cherry Lake Publishing would like to acknowledge the work of the Partnership for 21st Century Learning. Please visit www.p21.org for more information.

Printed in the United States of America
Corporate Graphics
July 2016

HOW-TO LIBRARY

TABLE OF CONTENTS

Build Your Skill!

You can use crochet to create amazing, colorful designs.

Crochet (pronounced "croh-SHAY") is a French word that means "hook." Crocheting is the craft of making soft fabric by hooking loops of yarn together.

There are many different ways to make crafts from yarn. Some popular techniques include knitting, braiding, weaving, latch hooking, and needlepoint. Like these other ways of crafting, crocheting allows you to use one simple stitch over and over again to make something amazing! Depending on the yarn you use, you can create a delicate piece of lace or a big, chunky blanket.

It's fun to learn a new skill. You may not get the hang of it right away. But the more you practice, the better you'll get. It's even more fun to learn with a friend or a group of friends. Invite your pals over for a crochet party! You can help each other fix mistakes and get the hang of it together.

This book will teach you how to use a single crochet stitch. There are also double crochet stitches, triple crochet stitches, and many others. Build your basic skills here first. When you feel ready, you can seek out more advanced **patterns**. There's no limit to the fun things you can make!

Once you learn the basic hand movements for crocheting, you can try more advanced techniques.

The History of Crochet

Using very thin yarn, you can crochet unique earrings and other jewelry.

Historians have found evidence of yarn crafts that dates back thousands of years. But they don't know exactly when and where people started to crochet. Some historians believe that crocheting began in what is now the Middle East. Others believe it started in Asia. It may also have roots in South America.

Throughout history, people have used crochet to make helpful items such as fishing nets. Crocheters have made everything from potholders and hats to jewelry and art, as well as lace to decorate clothing. People probably used their fingers for the earliest crocheting. Hooks and other tools were invented later.

Crocheting became quite popular in the 1800s in Europe. That's when the first crochet patterns were published. Before that, a crocheter copied samples of someone else's work without specific instructions to follow.

In the mid-1800s, crocheted lace was popular in Ireland. When people left Ireland to move to America, they brought their crocheting skills with them. Then crocheting became popular in America, too.

A warm, cozy blanket is useful and easy to make.

Which Yarn?

Walk into any yarn store and you'll see hundreds of types of yarn to choose from. You can often find yarn in craft and hobby stores, too.

Yarn comes in a **skein**—a bundle of yarn with a label around the middle. The label will tell you what the yarn is made of. You'll notice that various types of yarn feel different. Some are very soft, while others have a rougher **texture**. Yarn is made from either natural or **synthetic fibers**, or a combination of both. Natural fibers include cotton, which comes from plants, or wool, which comes from sheep. Synthetic yarns are created from artificial fibers, such as acrylic or polyester.

Yarn comes in almost any color you can imagine.

Different types of yarn require different kinds of tools.

The label also tells you the weight of a yarn. Very thin yarns are labeled "super fine." Very thick ones are labeled "super bulky." It is best to choose a medium-weight yarn if you are just learning how to crochet.

You may see a number stamped on the label. This is the yarn's dye lot. If you are buying more than one skein for a project, make sure they are all from the same dye lot. This means they were dyed at the same time, so the color will be the same. Not all yarns are dyed one color. Some are a mix. Some yarns are even jazzed up with glittery threads, ribbon, or other fun details. These are called novelty yarns.

Finally, the label tells you the size of the crochet hook needed to work with that yarn. Turn the page to learn about crochet hooks and other materials you will need to get started.

Basic Tools

A crochet hook is your most important tool. Hooks come in sizes ranging from small 0.75 mm (millimeter) hooks to large 20 mm ones. They are made of metal, plastic, bamboo, or wood.

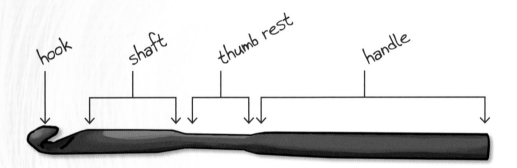

hook   shaft   thumb rest   handle

You will also need the following tools for the projects in this book:

- **_Stitch markers_**—These small plastic loops are a good way to mark rows or rounds. They are sold at yarn stores. You can also use safety pins instead.

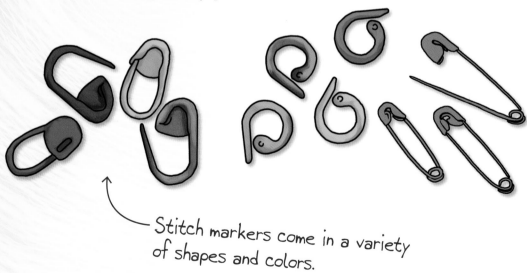

Stitch markers come in a variety of shapes and colors.

- **Scissors**—This is a necessary tool for cutting yarn.
- **Tape measure**—This is a flexible ruler used to measure yarn and fabric.
- **Paper and pencil**—These supplies are useful for planning designs or keeping track of stitches.
- **Tapestry needle**—This needle looks like an oversized sewing needle with a rounded tip and an **eye** that is large enough for yarn. It is useful for sewing in loose ends or piecing together parts of your crochet projects.

Other supplies for the projects include:
- Sewing needle and thread
- Felt
- Googly eyes
- Plastic pony beads
- Polyester fiberfill stuffing

MAKE A BALL

Some yarn comes in a hank instead of a skein. A hank is a long loop of yarn folded and twisted together. If you buy a hank, you'll have to wind the yarn into a ball before you start crocheting. If you don't, it will become a knotted mess!

Untwist the hank and keep the large loops of yarn together. Place the loops over the back of a chair. Wind the tail end of the yarn around your fingers about 10 times. Then take the loops off your fingers and start winding the yarn in the other direction so a ball starts to form. Continue winding the yarn around your ball. Turn the ball now and then, to make sure it stays round. The chair will keep the yarn from getting tangled.

Getting Started

Here are some basics techniques you will need to get started:

The Slipknot

A slipknot is the first step of every crochet project. It secures the yarn to your crochet hook. Your yarn has two ends—the tail (the cut end of the yarn) and the ball yarn (the yarn that leads to the ball).

1. Pull a piece of yarn from the ball and make a loop about 12 inches (30.5 centimeters) from the tail.
2. Slip your crochet hook into the loop. Use it to hook the tail yarn and pull it through the loop.
3. Pull gently on both yarn ends to tighten the knot onto the shaft of the crochet hook.

The Chain Stitch

The chain stitch is the most basic crochet stitch.
1. Hold the slipknot in place with your left thumb and middle finger.

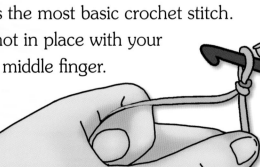

2. Wrap the ball yarn from the back to the front of the crochet hook. This is called yarning over. Turn the crochet hook to catch the yarn in the hook end.

3. Pull the yarn through the loop, so that the original loop comes off the shaft and the new yarn has made a loop on the shaft. You have made one chain stitch. Repeat as many times as needed for your project.

Secure the End

When you reach the end of a project, you need to secure the yarn so your stitches don't unravel. Cut the ball yarn about 12 inches (30.5 cm) from the end of your project. Then pull this yarn through the last stitch. Tug tightly to secure it.

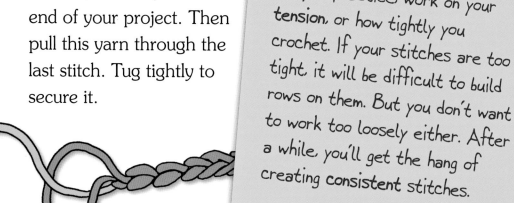

TOO TIGHT? TOO LOOSE?
As you practice, work on your tension, or how tightly you crochet. If your stitches are too tight, it will be difficult to build rows on them. But you don't want to work too loosely either. After a while, you'll get the hang of creating consistent stitches.

Hanging Icicle Chains

This project can help you practice your chain stitches. Pair your yarn with metallic thread or find a yarn that already has metallic thread running through it. Make lots of chains. Then hang them in a doorway for a soft and sparkly entrance.

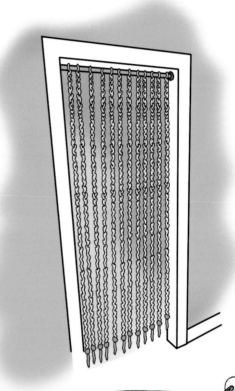

Materials

- Tape measure
- 1 skein white or light-blue medium-weight yarn
- 1 spool metallic thread
- Size 5.5 mm crochet hook
- Scissors
- About 30 sparkly plastic pony beads
- Tension curtain rod sized to fit in a doorway

Steps

1. Measure the height of the doorway.
2. Hold the yarn and thread next to each other as if they were one. Secure them to the crochet hook with a slipknot.

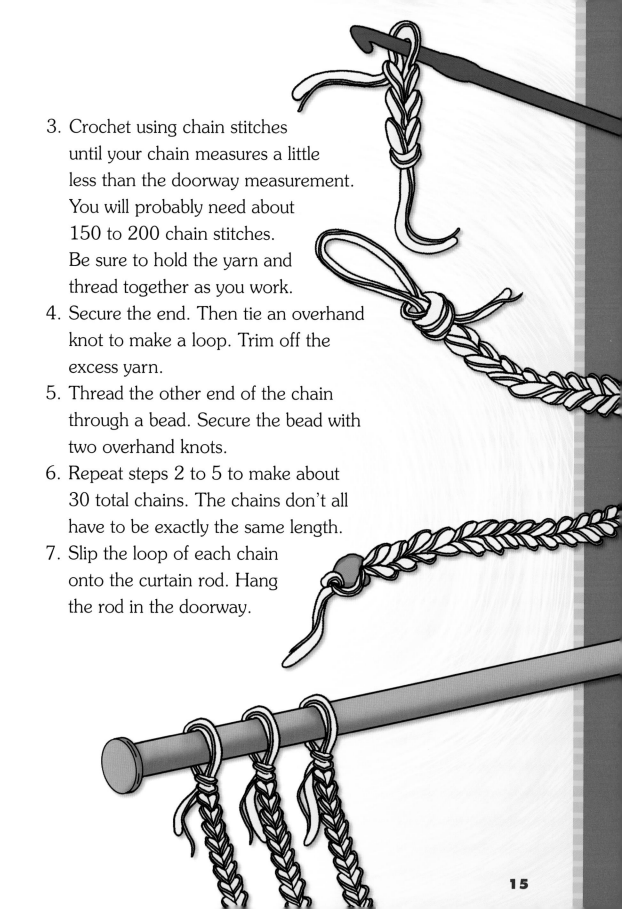

3. Crochet using chain stitches until your chain measures a little less than the doorway measurement. You will probably need about 150 to 200 chain stitches. Be sure to hold the yarn and thread together as you work.

4. Secure the end. Then tie an overhand knot to make a loop. Trim off the excess yarn.

5. Thread the other end of the chain through a bead. Secure the bead with two overhand knots.

6. Repeat steps 2 to 5 to make about 30 total chains. The chains don't all have to be exactly the same length.

7. Slip the loop of each chain onto the curtain rod. Hang the rod in the doorway.

Single Crochet Stitch

Build on your chain stitching skills by making rows of single crochet stitches.

To Build a Base Row

1. Secure the yarn to the crochet hook with a slipknot. Crochet 11 chain stitches. Hold the chain out from the top of the hook. You are going to work back across the chain stitches in the opposite direction.

2. You'll notice that each chain stitch looks like a little v. Skip the first chain stitch. Slip your crochet hook into the back of the v of the second chain stitch from front to back.

3. Yarn over with the ball yarn. Pull the yarn through to make a new loop on the crochet hook. Now you have two loops on your hook.

4. Yarn over again. Pull that yarn through both of the stitches on the hook. Now you have one new loop on the hook. You have just completed a single crochet stitch.

5. Slip the crochet hook into the back of the next chain stitch and repeat steps 3 and 4. Continue until you reach the end of the row. You should have 10 stitches. Count them by counting the v's across the top. Your base row is done!

To Make the Next Rows

1. Turn your piece so the crochet hook is at the start of the row again.
2. For this row, and the ones following, you don't need to skip the first stitch. Slip the needle under *both* parts of the v of the first stitch from front to back. Then repeat steps 3 and 4 on page 16. At the end of the row, count your stitches to make sure you didn't miss any. You should still have 10.
3. Continue crocheting as many rows as needed for your project. Secure the yarn at the end.
4. Use a tapestry needle to weave in the ends. Use scissors to trim the excess yarn.

Striped Bulky Lap Blanket

Single crocheting with this bulky yarn will make a cushy, warm, and cozy blanket to cover your lap on cold days.

Materials

- 6 skeins of super bulky yarn (3 in color A and 3 in color B)
- Size 11.5 mm crochet hook (or size suggested on yarn label)
- Tapestry needle
- Scissors

Steps

1. Secure the yarn to the crochet hook with a slipknot. Crochet 31 single chain stitches with color A. Then build a base row (see page 16). You will have 30 total stitches.
2. Continue making rows with color A until you get near the end of the skein (about 9 to 10 rows).

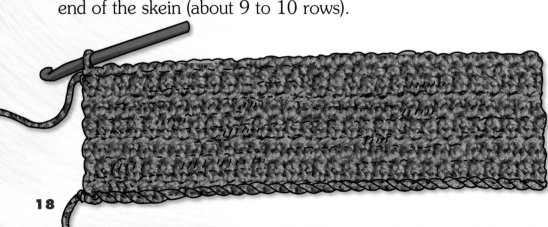

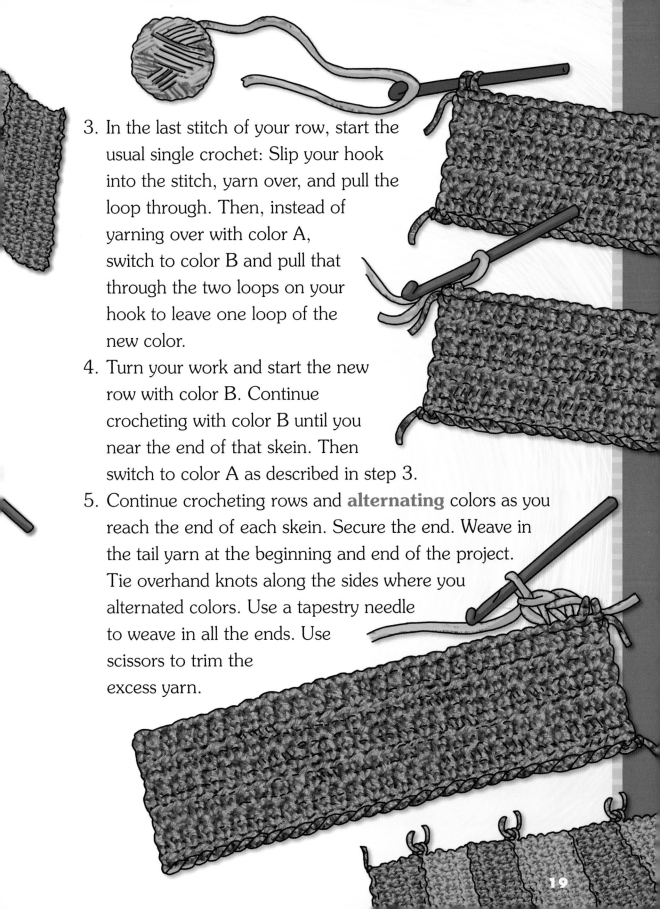

3. In the last stitch of your row, start the usual single crochet: Slip your hook into the stitch, yarn over, and pull the loop through. Then, instead of yarning over with color A, switch to color B and pull that through the two loops on your hook to leave one loop of the new color.

4. Turn your work and start the new row with color B. Continue crocheting with color B until you near the end of that skein. Then switch to color A as described in step 3.

5. Continue crocheting rows and **alternating** colors as you reach the end of each skein. Secure the end. Weave in the tail yarn at the beginning and end of the project. Tie overhand knots along the sides where you alternated colors. Use a tapestry needle to weave in all the ends. Use scissors to trim the excess yarn.

Soft Dice

These simple dice are made up of single-crocheted squares. Use them for any sort of game that requires regular dice. These are guaranteed to be softer and a lot more fun!

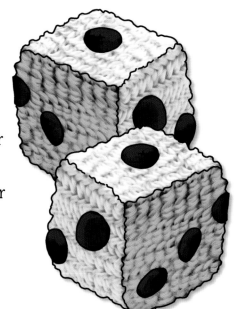

Materials

- 1 skein white medium-weight yarn
- Size 5.5 mm crochet hook
- Tapestry needle
- Scissors
- Polyester fiberfill stuffing
- 42 small black felt circles
- Black thread and sewing needle

Steps

1. Secure the yarn to the crochet hook with a slipknot. Crochet 11 chain stitches. Then build a base row (see page 16). You will have 10 total stitches.
2. Crochet 10 more rows to make a square. Secure the end, but don't weave in the yarn. Repeat steps 1 and 2 five more times to make six squares in all.

3. Using the tail yarn of the squares and the tapestry needle, sew two of the squares together. Then sew two more together. Then sew those sets of two together so that you have one long piece made up of four squares.

4. Sew the edge of the top square to the edge of the bottom square to make a box shape.

5. Sew the four sides of another square onto the top of the box.

6. Sew the last square onto the bottom of the box, but leave one of the sides open. Secure, weave in, and trim all the tail yarn.

7. Turn the box inside out. Fill it with stuffing. Sew up the last open side, secure it, and weave in the end.

8. Use the black thread and sewing needle to sew the felt circles onto the sides of your crocheted cube like the dots on a real die, from one to six.

9. Repeat all the steps to make a second die.

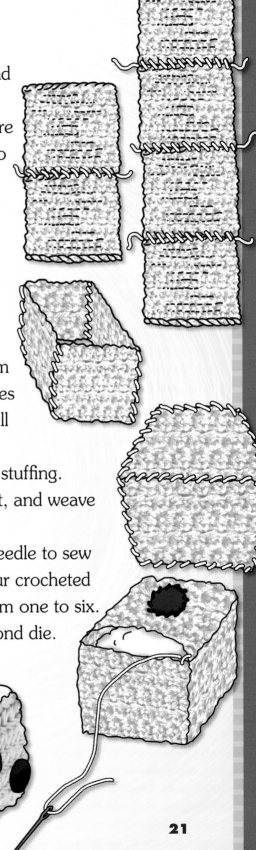

Monster Smartphone Case

Keep your cell phone safe inside this furry monster! This project will teach you how to crochet in the round instead of going back and forth in rows.

Materials

- 1 skein medium-weight yarn, any color
- Size 5.5 mm crochet hook
- Tape measure
- Tapestry needle
- Scissors
- White felt
- 2 googly eyes
- Tacky glue

Steps

1. Secure the yarn to the crochet hook with a slipknot. Crochet 21 chain stitches.
2. Slip stitch the two ends of the chain together: Slide the crochet hook into the chain closest to the slipknot. Hook the ball yarn with the hook and pull it through both loops so you have one loop on the hook.

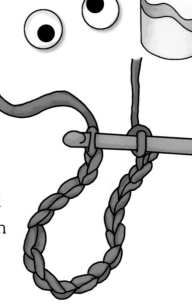

The chain should now make a circle.

3. Build a base round (remember to skip the first stitch) by single crocheting around the circle until you have 20 stitches. Be careful not to twist the circle as you work.

4. Continue crocheting around and around the circle. You don't have to worry about counting stitches. As you work, you will create a tube. Stop when your tube measures the length of your phone. Secure and weave in the end.

5. Use the tapestry needle to sew the tail yarn across the bottom edge to close up the bottom of the case.

6. Cut out two white felt triangles and glue them onto the front of your case. Then glue two googly eyes above them. Let the glue dry completely before slipping your phone inside.

Hexagon Crossbody Bag

Learn how to increase the number of stitches in each row as you crochet in the round. Fill this bag with a book, some treats, or balls of crochet yarn!

Materials

- 2 skeins medium-weight yarn in color A and B
- Size 5.5 mm crochet hook
- Stitch marker or safety pin
- Scissors
- Tapestry needle
- Pencil and paper to keep track of rounds and stitches

Steps

1. Secure the yarn to the crochet hook with a slipknot. Crochet four chain stitches. Slip stitch the two ends of the chain together (see page 22) to form a loop.
2. To build the base row, poke the hook into the center of the circle. Make a single crochet stitch.
3. Repeat this five more times. Rotate the circle with each stitch so you have six single crochet stitches around the circle. You should end up back where you started. Place a marker in the last stitch to mark the end of your round

Continue as
follows

4. ROUND 1: Crochet two times into every stitch. When you reach the end of the round, you will have 12 stiches in this round instead of 6. Move your marker to the last stitch.

   ROUND 2: Crochet into the first stitch, then crochet two times into the second stitch. Continue this pattern until you reach the end of the round. You will have 18 stitches total.

   ROUND 3: Crochet into the first stitch, crochet into the second stitch. Then crochet two times into the third stitch. Continue this pattern, crocheting twice into every third stitch, until you reach the end of the round. You will have 24 stitches total.

   ROUND 4: Two times every fourth stitch—30 stitches

   ROUND 5: Two times every fifth stitch—36 stitches

   ROUND 6: Two times every sixth stitch—42 stitches

   ROUND 7: Two times every seventh stitch—48 stitches

   ROUND 8: Two times every eighth stitch—54 stitches

   ROUND 9: Two times every ninth stitch—60 stitches

   ROUND 10: Two times every 10th stitch—66 stitches

   ROUND 11: Two times every 11th stitch—72 stitches

   ROUND 12: Two times every 12th stitch—78 stitches

   ROUND 13: Two times every 13th stitch—84 stitches

   ROUND 14: Two times every 14th stitch—90 stitches

   ROUND 15: Two times every 15th stitch—96 stitches

   ROUND 16: Two times every 16th stitch—102 stitches

   ROUND 17: Two times every 17th stitch—108 stitches

   ROUND 18: Two times every 18th stitch—114 stitches

   ROUND 19: Two times every 19th stitch—120 stitches

   ROUND 20: Two times every 20th stitch—126 stitches

5. Secure and weave in the tail yarn.

6. Repeat steps 1 to 4 with color B.

7. To make a strap, make a chain about 45 inches (114 cm) long with color A. Build a base row, then crochet one more row. Switch to color B at the beginning of the next row. Crochet two rows of color B, then secure and weave in the ends.

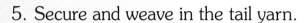

8. You'll notice that your hexagons have a front and back side. Lay the color A hexagon down flat with its front side down. Use a piece of color A yarn to sew one end of the strap to the inside of one of the hexagon's corners.

9. Lay the color B hexagon on top of the color A hexagon, front side up. Make sure the sides line up. Cut a 36-inch (91 cm) piece of yarn from color A. Starting at the corner near the strap, thread the yarn through all three layers (top hexagon, strap, and bottom hexagon). Knot it tight, then start sewing around the edges to join the hexagons. Stop when you have sewn four of the sides.

10. Insert the other end of the strap into the corner where you stopped sewing. Sew it to the inside of the color A hexagon. Secure and weave in all the ends.

Lacy Doily

This project is similar to the previous one, except you will use a much smaller needle and thin string instead of yarn.

Materials
- White cotton crochet thread
- Size 3.75 mm crochet hook (or size suggested on yarn label)
- Scissors
- Tapestry needle
- Stitch marker or safety pin
- Pencil and paper to keep track of rounds and stitches

Steps
1. Follow steps 1 to 3 of the Hexagon Crossbody Bag project.
2. Continue as follows:

    ROUND 1: Crochet two times into every stitch.
    You will have 12 stitches in this round.
    Move your marker to the last stitch.

    ROUND 2: Two times every second stitch
    —18 stitches

    ROUND 3: Two times every third stitch
    —24 stitches

    ROUND 4: Two times every fourth stitch
    —30 stitches

    ROUND 5: Two times every fifth stitch—36 stitches

3. Secure and weave in the ends.
4. Repeat steps 1 and 2 six more times to make seven hexagons in all. Lay out the hexagons with one in the center and the others lined up along its edges. Use the tapestry needle and crochet thread to sew around the center hexagon's edges to secure all the others in place. Knot the ends together when you reach the starting point. Weave in the loose thread and trim the ends.
5. Sew the edges between each **adjacent** hexagon. Secure, weave in, and trim the ends.
6. Add a single crochet around the outer edge of your piece. Start where two of the hexagons meet. Slip your hook into the v of the stitch, and single crochet all around until you end up where you started. Secure, weave in, and trim all the ends.

Start and finish here.

Single crochet all around the outside until you get back to where you started.

Feel the Rhythm

The more you crochet, the easier it will get. You may even notice that your hands will start moving in a regular rhythm as you slip the hook into a stitch, yarn over, pull through, yarn over, and pull through again. You won't even need to think about what you're doing!

After a busy day, you may find that crocheting can help you relax. So curl up in a cozy spot, grab your yarn and hook, and feel the rhythm. Try your hands at crochet!

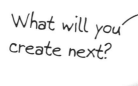

What will you create next?

Glossary

adjacent (uh-JAY-suhnt) close to or next to something

alternating (AWL-tur-nay-ting) going back and forth between two things

consistent (kuhn-SIS-tuhnt) always the same

eye (EYE) the hole at one end of a sewing needle

fibers (FYE-burz) thin strands of material

patterns (PAT-urnz) samples or models that can be followed as a guide

skein (SKAYN) a length or bundle of yarn

synthetic (sin-THET-ik) manufactured or artificial

tension (TEN-shuhn) the stiffness or tightness of something

texture (TEKS-chur) the way something feels

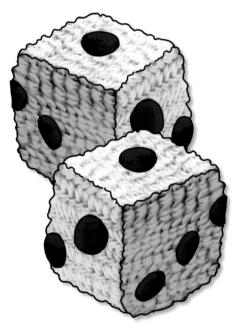

For More Information

Books

Davis, Jane. *Crochet: Fantastic Jewelry, Hats, Purses, Pillows & More*. New York: Lark Books, 2005.

Guy, Lucinda, and François Hall. *Kids Learn to Crochet*. North Pomfret, VT: Trafalgar Square Books, 2008.

Haab, Sherri, and Michelle Haab. *Way to Crochet! 20 Cool, Easy Projects for Kids of All Ages*. New York: Watson-Guptill Publications, 2006.

Ronci, Kelli. *Kids Crochet: Projects for Kids of All Ages*. New York: Stewart, Tabori and Chang, 2005.

Web Sites

Craft Yarn Council

www.craftyarncouncil.com/

Check out helpful tips and instructions for knitting and crocheting.

Crochet Guild of America

www.crochet.org

This site is full of information for beginner or expert crocheters.

Index

About the Author

Dana Meachen Rau is the author of more than 300 books for children on many topics, including science, history, cooking, and crafts. She creates, experiments, researches, and writes from her home office in Burlington, Connecticut.